T0067183

INNER
AWAKEN—TRANSFORMATION
CONSCIOUSNESS

INNER
AWAKEN–TRANSFORMATION
CONSCIOUSNESS

I Was Looking for Truth Love . . .
and Found Me?

DIANE P. BULLINS

edited by Brittany M. Stewart

Technical Support   Stepfon Cotton-Taylor

BALBOA.PRESS
A DIVISION OF HAY HOUSE

Balboa Press books may be ordered through booksellers or by contacting:

Balboa Press
A Division of Hay House
1663 Liberty Drive
Bloomington, IN 47403
www.balboapress.com
844-682-1282

Print information available on the last page.

ISBN: 978-1-5043-7470-5 (sc)
ISBN: 978-1-5043-7471-2 (e)

Balboa Press rev. date: 03/18/2021

Here is how a self pro claimed Wild
women's over emotional personality

Found the peace that she sought
by acclimatizing two enlightenment
trainings each with a Different insightful
approach. (similar however different.)

FOREWORD

I am writing this information in the attempt to re awaken the many people who were was once awaken by an enlightenment training and have returned to spiritual unconsciousness behavior. AKA spiritual Amnesia and what is acknowledged as earth consciousness. (Spiritually asleep consciousness)

*Most importantly. The attempt to awaken self to the fact that it is Spirit and to the people who are waiting to be validated that the occasional intuitive experiences is not mental illness.

(people who are new to self-awareness.

DISCLAIMER

In all of my experiences did I ever hear that EST is a religion What I did hear was EST is NOT a religion when anyone ask that question.

APPROACH # ONE PHILADELPHIA, PA.

Early June nineteen eighty one

I was down town in Philadelphia, Pa when I saw someone that I had not seen or Heard from since nineteen seventy-five MARY! We met when the two of us worked closely together at a prestigious teaching hospital in Philly as license graduate professional Medication nurses. It was imperative that we trusted each other absolutely. We were surprised and excited to see each other again. We decided to sit down and have coffee and to catch up on our present time lifestyle. Mary had finally married. I remembered that she was a joy to be around. Mary seemed to have a glow of amusement surrounding her. With a twinkle of merriment radiating within her clear blue eyes. Mary seemed preoccupied. at this time. I commented on her distraction Mary told me that she had something that she wanted to share with me that was very important to her lifestyle. I said, "tell me" then she asked me a question" "Diane have you heard 'of Werner Erhard and the EST training?" and the EST seminars? "no" I replied. Then she began to explain to the best of her ability. What I heard was abstract and rigid. When she was finish, I was a little confused and I told her that. As well as intrigued. I was then invited to one of her weekly evening (continuing education seminars) where she was certain I would get a better explanation and understanding. We set a date. On the evening of our agreement, Mary picked me up and she drove us to our destination.

When we arrived, I was led in the opposite direction from Mary. The room that was waiting for me was a modest size conference room, which was set up with, chairs all facing a podium and there was a small gathering of seminar enrollee's loved one and friends. They were there to get a better understanding just as I was there to do as well. We were asked at 8pm exactly to be seated and we were introduced to the speaking hostess of the evening. She was a petite pixie like female who had black hair and a radiant smile. She also had the talents of charm laced with amusement. She began to explain that she was in a program (GSLP) guest seminar leadership program. Designed to prepare her and others as well on how to give a better explanation why we were there. I heard the story of who Werner Erhard is and how he discovered a process on achieving possibilities. of living our wildest dreams into manifestation... I was immediately lit up with enthusiasm when I heard that there was a possibility to control my emotions? I also heard that there was the possibility to live my life differently. To learn to live our lives with the possibility of living our wildest dream goals into manifestation. Just in the process of life itself. Living possibilities? The training was designed for two weekends fully. I was so lit up that I was more than eager to find out where the next EST training would be in the Philadelphia area. I signed up for the June 21st 1981 training. I left with absolute certainty that this was something; I was waiting for most of my life. Two weeks before the training was scheduled. I received a telephone call, which was to inform me there was a mandatory pre- training meeting to share routine rules and regulations to prepare us for the rigid change. My information of rules and regulations that would prepare me for the rigid change of our expectations and of our new life experiences. I used the term rigid change because my personality was not ready for structure at that time. I lived my life habitually late and totally unaware of broken agreements. Integrity? What was that? Living out of my life experience of the training. We went over the most important ground rules, then onward to serious and important rules. The issue for me was what I could get from my very own training experience. Day one of EST training in Philadelphia Pa June12th, 1981. The first weekend I remember sitting in my chair looking around and wondering to myself quietly... "What the hell was I doing sitting among 200 perfect strangers?" that I had no trust experiences? We may have started on the 1st day strangers. By day two many of us were all in love with each other as well as our very own selves. My entire experience from the beginning to the end of the training was completely Spiritual! Unconditional love comes to mind. The trust that we gave to each other. I came in with trust issues. And I released that crippling emotion/vibration effortlessly. Everyone would get from the training whatever they desired and needed to improve their lifestyles or what would be needed to go forward as in manifesting their very own possibilities.

June twenty-first nineteen eighty-one GRADUATION NIGHT Graduates invited guests of the participants as well as old graduates to welcome us new comers. There were announcements and I heard two words ASSISTANT PROGRAM I was curious and I asked about the assisting program. Well I did not know how unconscious I was about charity. I was so unconscious toward giving of my time freely. When I heard that assistants were volunteering. I rudely commented saying "that is stupid." at that timed I would never do that I said" what I believed was true for me, and the truth will set you free. Because I left graduation night signed up to be communicator for my very own evening weekly seminar. I was not coerced I was given the opportunity of choice. This is my first proclaim that I am a communicator for Devine Mind.

Here is what I was required to do. I was to attend each and every seminar and write the most Pertinent Information. Clear with the seminar leader before leaving to make certain that I had the most important message given to enrollees. I would also check the attendance sheets and make phone calls to all absentees, before the next seminar. give them the seminar information then get a renewed agreement to continue the seminar series. I loved assisting so much that I learned other assistant duties. I was trained as receptionist (holding the space for enrollment calls to flow into the center). I was cashier for other seminars as well as for my own seminars series I did logistics (keeping the bath room meticulously clean... and running the mic at other trainings and my most enjoyable Assistance position was to act as greeter at the monthly special guest seminars the monthly special guest seminar. This where is where a trainer was the guest speaker. They taught the training sessions and who better to speak to our loved ones and invited guests?

I noticed while I was involved in the assistant program I was evolving spiritually and dropping my personalities' anger' charge buttons. I was becoming less emotionally charged around anger issues.

APPROACH TWO

Emeryville 1986

This is how I discovered the most compassionate, nurturing and dedicated transformation consciousness Educators in my truth love encounters. GREAT My next step into spiritual growth.

Emeryville, California 1986

September 1986 I was living one of my possibilities which was a dream goal of mine to experience working with my dad, who is a world renown playwright and author and educator. I had become the producers' assistant at the BMT theatre which was an off broad way theatre nonprofit production company. I was new to the area and I decided to check out the area since I loved to walk. one day I was out walking. I did not realize that I had left Emeryville and to my amazement I was on Shattuck avenue a main throughway in down town Berkeley, Ca. I had walked to another city.!

.. . .

I noticed that that there were many man newspaper box and most were free! I found out later that free was normal in this part of Berkeley. I was tired from my long strolling and I decided to sit on a bench at a bus stop. This is when I noticed a free news paper box marked SPIRITUAL RIGHTS FOUNDATION! I Remembered thinking "Why the Spiritual Rights? and what is it?" I could not resist looking at that box. I finally felt compelled to check out that newspaper. On the front page I learned that this paper was dedicated to all things pertaining to spirit! great the next step in my quest for truthful knowledge. The newspaper was published by Spiritual Rights Foundation/the seminary Academy for psychic Studies. Located in Berkeley.

Publisher William H. Duby. On the front page was advertised free healing clinic. I continued to read the paper cover to cover. There I read that there was FREE aura/energy healings Monday evenings. I knew that I would go just to experience exactly what this meant. One Monday evening September 1986. I set out to walk to the academy for psychic studies alone and without telling anyone where I was going. (suppose this was a hoax?). When I arrived at the address that was listed in that newspaper. I sure was nervous. All things pertaining to spirit? Huh? Well, I rang the rang the bell anyway and went in. The process was very organized and I had my healing and more information to my questions. answered quickly. Afterward I walked around. I saw a bulletin board advertising meditation and energy healing classes for anyone interested. I was really interested. In healings. These are called The begging classes I signed [up to take meditation #one. a six week one evening class for a small donation. After meditation #one I of course I took meditation #two. After that I was hooked I really was interested in healings and I completed healing one and healing# two. You may want to understand that these classes and experiences helped me to understand and acclimatize both enlightenment trainings that and what my personal purpose and helped me to come forward into present time about truth love.

The following are my very own interpretation of transformation consciousness observed from both trainings.(my own translations).

I am writing the following words that may explain transformation consciousness.

I call this SPIRIT TALK/ TRANSFORMATION LANGUAGING DEFINITION

AURA- aka electromagnetic field
This energy field surround every live being such as
People

Animals

Trees

PERSONALITY- The personality is your persona your façade your act. The who or what you see when you when you look into the mirror You are not your personality. The personality come with emotion (feelings) and earth consciousness aka your body. You are not your body which also mean you are not your emotions. Be aware that your personality will fight to be in charge over the self. (spirit).

You have emotions and this means that you can experience anger and you can choose not to act out emotions. ex. someone pushes your anger button you can observe that you are in anger/upset

You do not have to act out anger. You can be in amusement and not cuss out or get into an altercation of any kind. your choice. You are self/spirit.

NUTRALITY-control over the emotions aka over riding emotional charges. This vibration//emotion is very difficult for people//personalities to maintain. Because there is no good or bad no right or wrong. There is no judgement no good or bad no right or wrong in this state of transformation consciousness. ex. how neutral could you be as the betrayed friend or spouse? You plan to forgive the deceitful act. However loved ones and friends are constantly telling you to forget that person they don't deserve you. Consider that you have learn the benefits of living in neutrality and the people around you constantly want you to divide your loyalty. Ex. You are expected to choose sides which situation is right or wrong? You are being constantly harassed to demonstrate your loyalty. EVERY DAY. especially between step members and biological off springs (whew).

MISPERCEPTIONS- these are lies, deceit designed to trick, hoodwink, or disillusion as well or to ensnare the self into creating reasons and excuses for the personality to be in control. EX. You have an agreement to be on time for a very important interview and you wake up late. Your personality will blame everything and or everyone around you. The truth is you are in doubt and disbelief that you deserve this prestigious position. This interview is the next achieving next step in obtaining your dream goal manifested my next step in obtaining one of your dream /goal manifestations as well as releasing fear of successes. You wake up late (broken time agreement).misperception blames everything and everybody. The truth is This is your very own personality's doubt and disbelief that you are deserving of this great job. Experience. Because of over sleeping you miss out on keeping your time agreement and cancels the interview. Blaming the clock. (misperception.) blame excuses and reason for the personality to be right.

SACRED MIRRORS-The self's (spirit's) inner reflection Judge and know that you are judging yourself

(IT TAKES ONE TO KNOW ONE reflections)

EX. YOU ARE FACING SOME ONE that society deems very powerful and you are in awe of them, just so that you know you are looking at yourself. also when you are

In judgement of someone that you feel that should be frowned upon guess what? You are looking at yourself. Just because you are not acting out negative behavior it does not mean that it is not in your personality trait to experience one day. Or to show your personality's true nature. Judge and become what you have judged. You already have that for you to experience one day. It is already there in your personality. You can only see what is within yourself. Aka your closet behavior.

The word energy is sibling act and most people have acted out anger and every action that you re act to.

Some people have a sweet act, the goody too shoe act, etc.

THE WORD SPIRIT IS INTERCHANGED OFTEN WITH ENERGY. If you have heard these words. On the energy level

You were hearing On "the spirit level. You were in the presence of a transformation conversation

The word energy level is substituted because personalities get freaked out hearing "evil spirits"

Un clean energy aka evil spirits.

KARMA- is not pay back (think of it as YOU REAP WHAT YOU SOW)

The universe is designed to return whatever is planted into it whether it is earth soil or Devine Substance. EX. You plant apple seeds into the ground the seeds from the apple. The soil of the earth return back to you apples not peaches.

Universal ethers aka the invisible Devine substance. If someone plants intentional harm(thoughts toward another those negative intentions will be returned to the sender. It is not pay back. It is universal law. It makes no difference what it is. If it I planted evil thoughts into the universal ethers or earth soil it will return whatever was planted. it does not matter. The universal return back to the sender. It may not be immediate however the earth soil have been determined by earth time and season. Universal law does not have set patterns as crops planted.

I often hear people say "God don't like ugly it is not God doing pay back or vengeance it is you reap what you sowed.

ABANDONMENT ISSUES- Your momma did nothing wrong. She helped give you a body

That is healthy and beautiful. The spiritual contract between the two of you appears that you are to experience becoming adopted by a loving person or loving people. Your challenge seems to be to find forgiveness toward this situation before your death This is what has happened. Your personality took over (self/spirit) and acted out resentment to the extent of hatred. Know this personality agreement. (misperception over the self).your spiritual contract agreement is to embrace unconditional love. If you can do this You will receive Blessings abound. (spiritual agreement and if not you will experience struggle and effort your choice. I hope this will help you to awaken to your own inner awakening.

RELATIVES AND FAMILY – There are times in your personality experiences when you have thought to yourself I must be in the wrong family because the people that you were born among seem not to have anything in common with behavior and or expectations that you agree with. This is a spiritual challenge agreement. You chose these personalities before you took a body so that you could experience certain behaviors and this is designed for you to experience as a learning tool. This is your neutrality tests to conquer.

Neutrality contd

ayed friend or lover? You want to forgive this act of betrayal but your friends and love ones Continually remind you and have judged your friend or lover by saying" don't go back into that relationship you're too good for them forget them". The betrayed spouse you want to keep your marital vows but loved ones and friends think they know what is best for you. What should you do? Obey your marriage vows? Or give into the pressure. You can see how the neutrality vibration can be difficult. In my life the most pressure comes from my spouse who is a fault finder, constantly back stabbing. This is something that I struggle to with to maintain my neutrality space. My neutrality space is my ministers' space. What a struggle moment to moment daily. I try to resist and it is a constant battle to remain neutral. Very often moment to moment.

RESISTENCE- What you resist will persist. I f there is a worrisome situation in your life that you repeat experiencing that you constantly try to avoid experiencing.

This situation will continue to re appear in your life. Until you are able to dissolve the emotional charge surrounding this issue. Or topic. If you will continue to try to avoid this situation. The resistance will repeat continually. Until you wake up or are ready to stop this with unconscious behavior and change the behavior pattern. Ex. You keep attracting the same type of relationship behavior the partner that you seem to attract like it is their duty to beat you as the way to end altercations. You wonder why ? Until you stop resisting this behavior type it will continue until you dissolve the emotional charge (fear of the same, the same but not always choices in a relation ship. You will continue to attract this behavior pattern in relationships.

PERFECTION- ABSOLUTE TRUTH you are perfect just as you are. You are on planet earth.

In the process of becoming a spirit in a body SSPIRITUAL AMNESIA takes place.

HERE is an unusual example. Before taking a body you as spirit committed to fourteen other spirits to help to give them bodies and the only way to keep these promises is to give birth as mother. You are spiritually unconscious. Once you are born you keep those agreements. You have given birth to fourteen babies some by more than one dad. On earth you are gossiped about you are invalidated made to feel ashamed. In the spiritual consciousness you are a super success. you kept your spiritual agreement. You helped fourteen other spirits get to planet earth with perfect bodies nothing less. This is an unusual situation it takes a strong as well as A stubborn personality. I personally am connected to two such personalities Marie Mae Kittrell Bullins (my birth mother) and Karen Mary Taylor (my birth daughter good job ladies. I was in a state of spiritual amnesia aka genetic body programing I gave my Karen hell but she refused to abort her pregnancies. I stand corrected. since learning the absolute truth. I now know that every person have a spiritual contract to live out. This is where agreements are kept or not kept. (choice) free will.

remember you are here acting out earth consciousness behavior beliefs.

ENERGY- In the conversation of transformation. Energy. are Thoughts, Vibrations, emotions and the invisible (controversial) energy known as Universal Devine Mind Christ Consciousness.

PERSONALITY TRAITS UNCONSCIOUSLY ACTED OUT WHILE IN THE STATE CALLED SPIRITUAL AMNESIA

DOUBT and DISBELIEF This personality goes through life acting out that they are not good enough to enjoy the better things that life have to offer.

This personality live with the mentality of reason which says that if it is outside of the five physical senses then it does not exist these are the doubting Thomas syndrome.

(science)-earth consciousness.

LACK and LIMITATIONT this personality worry, worry and worry that they do not have enough of. whatever they think that they need for survival. If it's money this personality have been known to experience a panic attack. Even to simply shop at the local .99- $1.00 store. If it's food I have seen refrigerators over flowing with left overs because of the inability To waste food or money.

STRUGGLE and EFFORT- This personality is known to enjoy working laborious Jobs and enjoy receiving a pat on the back for a job well done for less than top dollar.

They seem to live out the no pain no gain syndrome.

I have lived out struggle and effort. Raising two babies while working part time as a nurses' aide and going to school full time to become a license practical nurse and I own these actions victoriously. This was perfect for my personality at that time. I was also acting

out doubt and disbelief. I did not receive
my high school diploma the traditional
way I earned my high school diploma
by way of GED. Which was my destiny.
Numerology describe my personality as a
healing woman. I was a nurse's aide before
certification existed, a license practical
medication nurse. And in present time
I am Aura aka spirit healer (aura healer).
And a minister of the healing arts.

I consider my spiritual mission as COMMUNICATOR
FOR DEVINE MIND CHRIST CONSCIOUSNESS
ONE OF MANY people.

I HEARD THAT In September of 1990 Werner
Erhard would release a paradigm a milder

Form of the EST training to be given in San Francisco
California and I was there among a room filled with EST
graduates and other scholars. I know this because I went
around and introduced myself and ask several people that

was present. What there reason for being there. I did not commit to the forum by participating in activities offered by the FORUM STAFF. In present time I have

Re considered and I am planning to participate actively in the FORUM activities. There seems to be new I depth of information that I want to learn and act out as I have evolved to another level of comprehension.

PERFECTION- THE TRUTH

You are perfect just the way that you are The following scenario is unusual in the earth consciousness behavior.

Note: every experience that you suffer and or experience is perfect for your spiritual growth. And to prepare your personality for the next step in your life plan. Consciousness behavior. Before taking your body you gave a spiritual agreement to help give bodies to fourteen other spirits. The only way to honor those agreements is to give births as mother. On earth you have kept your agreements even with more than one birth dad.(several

You are scorn gossiped about in earth consciousness behavior. On the spirit level you

Are a super success you have kept your spiritual goal agreement and you have helped fourteen spirits em bod y. This is not the normal earth behavior. It is a spiritual

Level agreement I know two females personally who accomplished. This courageous feat

GOOD JOB LADIES- Marie Mae Kittrell Bullins (my birth mother).and

Karen Mary Taylor (my birth daughter).

NOBODY IS BETTER THAN ANYONE ELSE-WE ARE ALL SPIRITS/SOULS

TRYING TO AWAKEN TO OUR TRUE PURPOSE (OUR SPIRITUAL AGREEMENT.)

THOUGHTS AND WORDS- These are real things and CAN and DO take up residency in your electromagnetic field (aka your energy field or aura).

THE BOX DWELLERS-These are the people try to control people behavior.

If you have heard think outside of the box. Aka the invisible box of society's code of ethics.

(the invisible box) that society try to rule everyday situations

What is common decency

What is decent behavior

-judgmental attitudes

Causes of gossiping

All of this is earth conscious behavior which is the root causes of spiritual asleep consciousness.

Integrity- find the definition for integrity and try to live your life style to as close to that word.

RESPONSIBILITY- SPIRITUALLY AWAKE BEHAVIOR

The truth is what works

Keeping your word- agreements keep power over the personality

IRRISPONSIBILITY – IS OF EARTH CONSCIOUSNESS –SPIRITUALLY ASLEEP BEHAVIOR

Lies

Deceit

Broken agreements

Lateness is a broken agreement and lessens power over the personality.

To bear false witness- To believe a rumor about someone or a situation that you have not experienced yourself is to believe a lie.

Ex. In my experience my spouse is constantly trying to get me to believe the things that teens can do. He has no proof just speculations. We can and do get into disagreements because if I have not experienced these speculations with my own eyes. I cannot believe them. It can be frustrating trying to remain in my neutrality space. So the challenge begins... speculations vs truth keeps self in control over the personality In this situation I'm referring to my two grand sons (ages 19 and 20)

They enjoy visiting live wie their dad my spouse and my 28 year old step son. David Anthony. The two college students are just completing their first year in college. There is no evidence of smoking anything nor do they disappear without telling of their intentions. They may very well be guilty of teen activities. If they are guilty they hide it very well. I am not naïve; I raised their dad and he was no goody too shoes and their aunt Karen Mary. Those two were a handful and I had a stepdaughter Barbara Ann. You can trust the fact that I know suspicious teen behavior. Speculations continue and I am maintaining my neutrality.

Find the definition of integrity and act it out often

WHO IS REV DI COMPARED TO THAT SELF PROCLAIMED WILD WOMAN?

October 2018. I am very grounded in the fact that I am self-awakened as spirit. As I am writing this book it is completely humbling because I am 100% positive that I have re awakened from the state of spiritually asleep consciousness again recently. I am a ordained minister licensed by the state of California and I have not been doing what I promised The Living God that I would do.

I graduated as a minister on February28th,2010. I became associate minister for Spiritual Rights Foundation dedicated to help awaken personalities from spiritual amnesia as well as act out spiritual rights. We are spirits and we have rights. and I am aware that I have allowed my personality to distract my spiritual intentions. My choice. unconscious or not I have not done what I absolutely love to do which is attend healing clinics or do the other ministers' duties that I was privileged to learn to do. Just because I know that I am ready to release the energies that my personality was responding to. I have returned to healing clinic occasionally. I am conscious that I had fallen back into spiritually unconsciousness and remember daily that I am perfect just as I am. I was destine to return to spiritual unconsciousness so that I will have compassion for others who may do the same. Once again I reiterate NEUTRALITY is very difficult to maintain.

A I have received healings and I am aware where I allowed the personality to take over and when I say neutrality is very difficult to maintain and that the personality will fight to be in control.

This is very possible and I am aware of this daily. I love, love love giving aura/spirit healings

I give healings to my family members @ home when they want to cooperate

THE PERSONALITY KNOWN AS Diane P. Bullins

NOTE; I HEARD THAT Werner Erhard was teaching a milder paradigm of the EST training In

September 1990 I was sitting there along with many others however I did not commit as I did the EST TRAINING In present time I plan to participate in the FORUM activities.

My personality can be described as over bearing outspoken and a loud mouth and long after the EST training I continued to experience no control over my emotions. I recognize my personalities' tendency to have rage and a fiery temper. I did act out physically (having fist fights) with neighborhood men and win. until I found myself in a situation where I had to defend my honor on my own. without protection or loyalty of my husband at that time I had married a man who was in sympathy with the neighbors just to keep the peace ct did not matter that jealousy was rampart toward us. I had my own car and money to spend e and I felt that it was not a good idea to gossip with neighbors and I found out later I was considered a snob and called uppity behind my back. I found this out when I had to beat down my next door neighbors adult son when he began to spread all kinds of nonsense about my character and his idea of what I did when I left in my own car. My reputation preceded me after that. (after I whupped his butt.) I had altercation of all kinds until I left Philly in 1986. I discovered SRF and learned about neutrality. I try very diligently to remain in my neutrality space especially in present time.

It is difficult to have to monitor your emotions moment to moment. But I no longer have altercations often. Occasionally someone who cannot get a emotional attack from me will try to p push my buttons. It is to have me act out anger and now my new identity is goody too shoes. what a joke. me? Goody too shoes? and yes I am Revdi and I have a personality that I have consciously acclimated with the self.

I do not care as long as long as I am in amusement about how I handle anger. My intentions with This book is transformation understanding. I pray that you gain some insight from my experiences. Really my personality is far from boring or goody too shoes. Fortunately I I.

am about to share something that is very, very personal however is public record (2) things in fact.

a. In 1968 I did not graduate with my high school class instead I chose to give birth to my son who is now known as PhD –Dr. Steph B. Taylor his degree is in environmental health and occupational safety. This means that I am classed as high school drop out although I did obtain my GED. And continued on to get my practical nursing license in 1974. And I became a professional medication nurse as well as a charge nurse eventually. (my experience with struggle and effort-b. I in2005 I stood up at a AA meeting and announced that I was a alcoholic. I have not regretted that decision because since january27,2005 I have been alcohol free! What a relief.

I reiterate my personality was no goody too shoes.

In present time I am a ordained minister licensed by the state of California and I am a healer of the aura as well as spirit I love love love giving healings. This is part of my transformation training experience. I will always be a healer of aura and a healer of spirit and I do aura healings and aura readings @ home etc.

About TRUTH LOVE

I was looking for truth love and found me! My personality was constantly beating herself f up

And I was in self destruct mode. The discovery of both approaches of enlightenment trainings led me to who and what I am known as in the here and now. My sincere thanks to Rev William H Duby/ SRF Inc.

Werner H. Erhard/EST/ land mark forum world wide

I write to re awaken others who are ready to participate again in the game of life at a High level. of participation You know who you are. I look forward to playing with you too.

Unconditional to accept my flaws as well as my goodness. To love the mistakes that my personality have made along the way to my life understanding in the here and now This is how I found me. Rev Di. Aka Rev Diane P. Bullins. I earned my prefix which is Revern. I am

Rev Di.

This is my earned (theological name.)

HELLO!

THE IMAGINATIONI- in earth consciousness the imagination is considered childlike. I can truthfully tell you the imagination" First, we cannot overload the human brain. This divinely created brain has fourteen billion cells. If used to the maximum, this human computer inside our heads could contain all the knowledge of humanity from the beginning of the world to the present and still have room left over. Second, not only can we not overload our brain - we also know that our brain retains everything. I often use saying that "The brain acquires everything that we encounter." The difficulty does not come with the input of information, but getting it out. Sometimes we "file" information randomly of little importance, and it confuses us."

When we use the imagination to manifest it is a very powerful tool.

and when it is accompanied with visualization have been observed to help manifest your intentions

THE SUBCONSCIOUS MIND- is a tool of infinite wisdom to help guide self/spirit.

It never sleeps it is a recording mechanism everything that we have ever heard or seen in our life time. It records from the instant conception occurs. This is why it is suggested singing and talking to unborn fetus. science refers to this unseen factor that the brain is doing the job of the subconscious mind. The imagination is a tool of the subconscious mind. In science it is said "hearing is the last to go." Spirit/ self knows that it is the function of the subconscious mind. When a person have been in medical coma have been known to awaken and have been able to relate conversations heard by staff members who are unaware of this information. It has been confused with functions of the brain only. In earth consciousness the imagination is not considered a function. Because it cannot be measured by the five physical senses.

Without becoming anger and choose not to act out. In other words you do not have to cuss out

The person or re act violently toward a situation. You can recognize that you are in anger or upset.

You can be in amusement and allow the emotion to dissipate. Your choice.

THOUGHTS AND WORDS- are real things and can and do take up residency in your energy field.

Ex. You are unaware that you have this very powerful and magnetic force surrounding your body. You have your own thoughts flowing. Some may be self defeating but not self destructive.

You are in a crowd of people who seem to like you. There are those who hide vicious thoughts

Toward you. You were in a positive radiant mood. Then you experience vibrations of doubt, failure and self destruct tendency.

a. You have attracted someone else's thought forms (e who may have unconsciously released toward you).

b. someone among you that truly want to see to your failure and purposely directed energy at toward you.

You are in spiritually asleep consciousness and you begin to act out these foreign energies as though these were your own thoughts.

NUTRALITY- This vibration is very difficult for personalities (people) to maintain.

In the state known as neutrality. There is no right or wrong good or bad. The following is an example of analogy - Before this female embodied from the infinite realm. She gave fourteen other spirits a committed agreement to help give them bodies. The only way to do this is to give physical birth as mother on earth. If She is to keep this enormous responsibility. On earth she is ridiculed invalidated, shunned. But in infinite consciousness she is a huge success she kept her spiritual agreement an helped give perfect bodies to fourteen babies. This is an uncommon situation and it takes a very strong and stubborn personality. The fact that she gave birth to these spirits there was no spiritual agreement to raise them all. All of these spirits have their own agreements to experience and this courageous female will be gossiped about because she gives some of these personalities their freedom to keep their own spiritual agreements. Some have spiritual agreements to be adopted. Others have agreements to be abandoned and to live their lives to find out that the birth mother did nothing wrong. Because neutrality is of the spiritual consciousness.

AKA Transformation consciousness.

These are other names used to describe transformation consciousness

DEVINE MIND

UNIVERSAL ETHERS

CHRIST CONSCIOUSNESS

THOUGHT FORMS

FOREIGN ENERGIES

AURA

CHAKRAS

EARTH CONSCIOUSNESS BEHAVIOR (A major NO-NO)

INVALIDATIONS; This action is to UNDER MIND ANOTHERS SELF ESTEEM

AND OR LESSENS THE CONFIDENCE OF OTHERS INTENTIONALLY

Her is more personal information of Diane P. Bullins' personality I enjoyed dirty dancing hence the name disco Di.(what earth consciousness)loose body movement in the 70's

Transformation consciousness is my passion and my love

1. And to reawaken others who have returned back to spiritual amnesia and or spiritually comatose

aka spiritually asleep consciousness/earth consciousness

2. To validate people who have been searching for this information.

To own who they are as spirits alive in a body.

Diane P. Bullins

RESPONSIBILITY- Spiritual behavior will include

Keeping agreements

Immediate acknowledgement when you slip out of neutrality

Punctuality keep time agreements

Learn what integrity living is for you

Charity- sharing what have been given to you with others that are in need

IRISPRISPONSIBILITY- Personality/ earth conscious behavior

Judgmental

Acting out your emotions without conscious thought

Anger

Ignoring those in need (the homeless) the hungry

"Ignoring people on the streets asking for change and you refusing to give them a dime.

Project

KARMA-The Universal LAW of you reap what you sow. This means that whatever thought or words with intention(plant)into the universal ethers Will boom arang back to you.

EX. You have thoughts of success of a project you will receive success. (If that is truly your desire)

You have fear of failure, and your project slowly becomes the failure of your fears.

This the universal law of Devine substance responding. It is not pay back or consequences

SYMBOLOGY: compare this to the earth soil and you have planted corn. You expect corn to grow you sowed c and you reap corn. You sow hatred you will receive hate back toward you. you.

You sow prosperous thoughts. You will receive prosperity. The word karma is needed in the earth consciousness mentality (spiritually asleep mentality) because the word karma has a Sense that in a Sense that it implies it is real to see. (Imagined pay back or consequences).

Karma is a universal law. The thoughts and or ideas that you conscious or unconsciously release

Will return to the sender (you). Therefore, you would be wise to watch your thoughts as much as you care about what happens to you.

GROWTH PERIOD

This is when self is ready to go forth to the next step in the spiritual agreement to experience

And the personality is unwilling to cooperate in giving up power to the self's next spiritual growth.

Ex. I was ordained and my next step was to learn to transcribe the concordant. I prepared the night before preparing my mode of transportation electrical powered wheel chair. And charging my cell phone. I set out with confidence. My chair's battery ran out of power enrooted meet with the person who was to teach me how to interpret the concordant. I tried to call and say that I would be late my cell phone ran out of power. When I finally arrived at my destination. I was teased. It was explained that I was in a growth period. I was stuck only two blocks from my destination my personality was very frustrated.

GROWTH PERIOD- This is when self/spirit need to go forward in the personality next spiritual achievement, and the personality rebels.

Here is one example: I had just graduated from ministers training and have been ordained. The next step for my enlightenment was to transcribe the bible by using the concordant. I had an agreement to meet with a upper graduate to learn how to do this and it was a homework assignment. I had the most ridiculous interruptions. On my way to keep my agreement. First. My power wheel chair ran out of power I had it charging for 24 hours so I started out on my journey confident.2nd my cell phone battery ran out of charge. When I tried to call and to say that my chair mal functioned and I would be late. I plowed forward to keep this very important agreement When I finally arrived I was laughed at because I was around the corner from my agreement and then it was explained to me that I was in a growth period. I was a winner over my personality. I did not give power over who I am. (self/spirit). This is one example of how easy the personality will try to ensnare you (self)? I did not panic or give up. I remained in neutrality.

It could have been so easy give up my power to the personality.(whew)!

HUMAN NATURE V/S PERSONALITY

I know that most of us have heard that is human nature when someone has done some awful misdeed or you see on the news some terrible conduct toward another person. The truth is Human Nature is The Christ Consciousness nature- kind forgiving and giving as well as charitable. The misperceptions are the nature of the personality aka (earth consciousness or e passing down the personality tree. You could be acting out genetic body programing of a race of people unintentionally and in a spiritually amnesia state. more often than not. The genetics of a serial killer from a family member that have never been mentioned (dark family secret) until it has been consciously wiped out) of the family history. And that should have been that should have been acknowledged. with the family hero. Or the fact that there is domestic violence tendencies In the genetic body programing. Or that a rapist tendency may be passed down through the generations to come.

SACRED MIRROR-When you are engaged face to face with another person you are in a spiritual reflection of yourself. The old saying" it takes one to know one" is absolute truth. You cannot see some else's flaw unless that flaw is in your consciousness (usually unconscious).

EX. You are experiencing jealousy from someone they are only reflecting your very own

Emotion from you. YES they are only picking up that emotion from you, yes you who will never admit that you are jealous, but all the females that you come in contact with is jealous of you?

You have jealousy in your emotional body programing. and you are spiritually asleep. I know plenty of you will say "Rev Di is so crazy. This may sound crazy and it is spiritually awake knowledge. You may want to check out when you find yourself judging someone else's social flaw that you your self is capable of. This is what I do when I find myself in judgement I immediately check my own self by saying to myself" what is this person reflecting back at me? Sometimes it's anger that I thought that I had released. I do acknowledge that it is me that I am experiencing. This is why practicing neutrality constantly is…spiritually empowering. REMEMBER. No one is better than anyone else is. Judge and you are probably what you have judged. YOU ARE PERFECT JUST AS YOU ARE

I am are here on earth to experience learning to overcome being a high school drop out

And the experience alcoholism and having a baby out of wedlock

I went through the shame of both of the above and I love my life.

I chose to give birth to my first born a healthy baby boy who weighed 8lbs 12ounces who now is PhD Dr Stephen B. Taylor his degrees are in environmental health and occupational safety. Stephen is constantly improving Osha outreach instructor and trainer. I write about his accomplishments o make my personality prideful because I dropped out of high school to give him life September 1990 I was sitting in a chair listening to Werner Erhard talk about a new paradigm called the Forum I found it to be a less rigid extension of EST. I did not continue

With the forum education at that time. I am now ready to participate. I have been studying the forum out and it is still thriving. It appears that it here to stay. I'm on my way to acclimatize. See you there!

enco-The Universal law of You reap what you sow

INVALIDATIONS- These are words of complaining, critizing and or

To cause confusion or strife toward a person or situation. EX. A love one says to you

"you were doing so well. What happened? Invalidations are so very wrong even when said

As a joke it lowerscauses self doubt and most of all push you out of your neutrality space.

VALIDATION- these are words of praises encouragement and causing confidence in another.

ENERGY: Transformation consciousness explains- aka spirit/ self

It is also your vibrations, thoughts and words can be included

Forein energy – some else's thoughts or body programing

Past time energy – dream goals that you once thought that you wanted to obtain

And changed your mi

Printed in the United States
by Baker & Taylor Publisher Services